The Really BIG Su

Sara Goodwins

Tram Tales of the  Manx Electric Railway

Loaghtan Books
Caardee
Dreemskerry Hill
Maughold
Isle of Man
IM7 1BE

Published by Loaghtan Books

First published: July 2018

Copyright © Sara Goodwins, 2018

Typesetting and origination by:
Loaghtan Books

Printed and bound by:
Latimer Trend

Website: www.loaghtanbooks.com

ISBN: 978-1-908060-21-1

All rights reserved. No part of this publication may be reproduced, stored on a retrieval system or transmitted in any form or by any means without prior permission of the publishers.

For all those who helped
with the resurrection of
Fenella Fourteen

Tram Tales of the Manx Electric Railway

1 Something on the Line
2 Stick to Safety
3 The Really Big Surprise

Author's note: Most of the events in *The Really Big Surprise* happened as described. However, Number 14 was not taken from Ramsey shed direct to Derby Castle. She was transferred by road to the Laxey shed, stored there for a time and made the rest of the journey to Derby Castle towed behind tramcar Number 33. In addition, tramcar Number 22 was rebuilt in 1992, so would have been able to take part in the cavalcade at the MER's centenary in 1993 (see page 23). Neither of these facts made such a good story, however...

CONTENTS

Chapter 1 'Happy Birthday to us.' **5**

Chapter 2 That night, before going to sleep... **8**

Chapter 3 But it wasn't. Next day... **10**

Chapter 4 That night, in the Derby Castle tram shed... **16**

Chapter 5 As Sven was working up and down the line... **18**

Chapter 6 The birthday party was getting closer... **22**

Chapter 7 At last the birthday party arrived. **25**

Chapter 8 The birthday celebrations were going to last a week... **27**

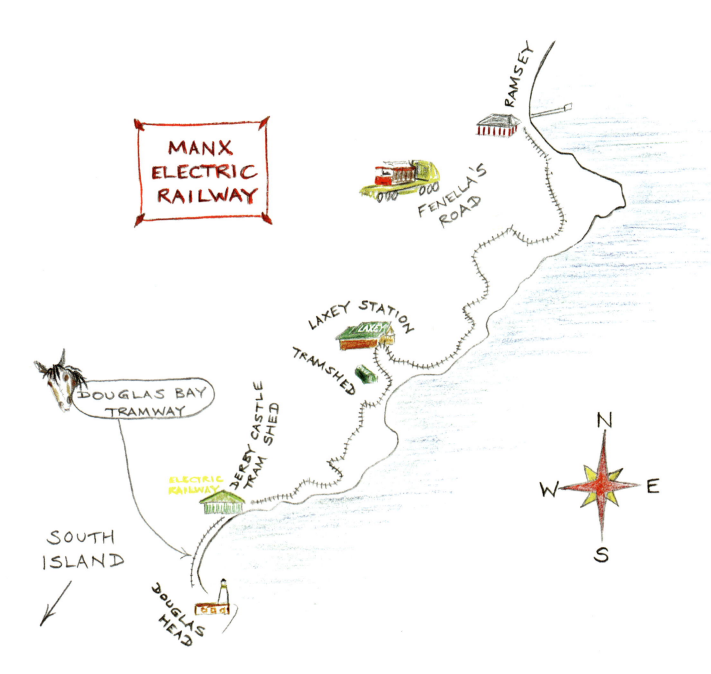

CHAPTER 1

'Happy Birthday to us,' sang Joan, the Number 2.

'Tum-te-tum-tum Tum Tum,' chirped Twain, the youngest tram, Number 22.

'Pom-pa-pom-pom Pom Pom Pom,' hummed Sven the Number 7.

'Happy Birthday to us!', warbled Pam the Paddlebox, Number 16.

Derby, the Number 1 and the Oldest Tram in the World, frowned a little. Yes, OK, it was lovely that the trams were going to be celebrating their 125th birthday very soon, but they still had work to do. Passengers had to come first. He rattled his pole to get everyone's attention:

'I know we're all excited,' he said, 'but, come on now, we have a service to run. Sven! You're on duty aren't you?' Sven stopped humming, blinked in surprise and hurried off with his crew.

Joan smiled fondly at Derby:

'Lighten up!' she whispered.

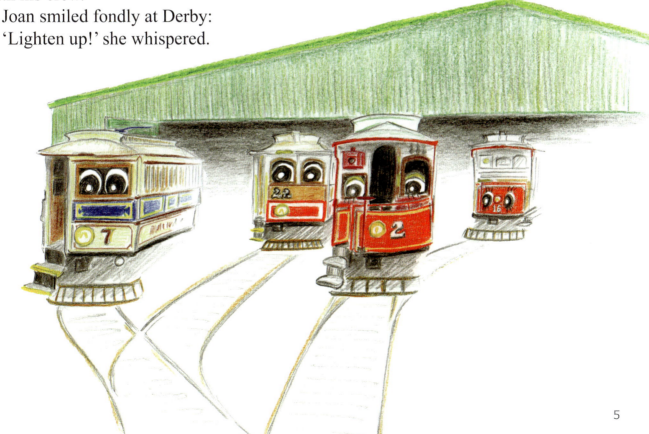

Sven coasted happily down from the Derby Castle tram sheds (named after the Number 1). 125 years! And a birthday party!

Sven was Number 7 and a tunnel car. That meant that he'd started life with long wooden seats running down either side of him so that his passengers faced

inwards. Not long ago his seats had been changed so that they faced forwards.

Sven was sad about losing his nice wooden seats and didn't find his new ones as comfortable, but he hadn't been asked whether he minded, so he just put up with it.

Sven and his crew shunted into place next to the ticket hut to wait for their passengers. Sven started humming again. A birthday party!

'Are you excited about the birthday party, Sven?' asked his Motorman.
'Oh yes,' said Sven. 'We usually get lots of visitors, and special things happen.'
'Well something really special is happening this time,' said his Motorman
'What's that?' said Sven excitedly.
'Oh I'm not going to tell you,' said his Motorman, 'it's going to be a Really Big Surprise.'

Sven wheedled and coaxed and pleaded, but his Motorman laughed and wouldn't tell him what the surprise was going to be. All he would say was that he was sure Sven – and all the other trams of course – would like it.

CHAPTER 2

That night, before going to sleep in the Derby Castle shed, Sven told the other trams about the Really Big Surprise. He still didn't know what it was, but he did know there was going to be one.

'Perhaps they'll re-open our old Ramsey station,' said Timothy Twenty. Lots of the trams looked hopeful.

'Perhaps I'll be painted green again,' said Pam the Paddlebox, who didn't like being red. Tina, her trailer, nudged her and Pam shut up quickly.

'Perhaps we're going to get a royal visitor,' called Regina the Royal Trailer from the back of the shed. Regina (Number 59) was very posh and had been built for Very Important People to ride on. She had even carried a King and Queen. Because of that she thought she was more important than most of the trams and *much* more important than all the other trailers. The rest took no notice; Regina was just Like That.

'No, no, no,' said Derby. 'It's much more likely that we'll be having a visit from Sutherland.' Sutherland was the Number 1 engine on the steam railway which went from Douglas to South Island. The only tram which had been on the steam railway was Thrust the Thirty Three. The trams couldn't ask Thrust about the steam line now, though, because he lived in Laxey shed.

'Oh yes, I remember Sutherland,' said Joan the Number 2. 'He's older than us and had his 125th birthday party in Laxey about twenty years ago.'

'That's right,' said Derby. 'I was a different colour then.' He looked rather meaningfully at Pam who blushed, and added, 'perhaps a visit from Sutherland is the Really Big Surprise.'

CHAPTER 3

But it wasn't. Next day Sven asked his Motorman whether Sutherland was visiting the tram line.

'No,' said his Motorman. 'None of the steam engines can get time off to visit.' Sven thought that was a pity.

As Sven worked up and down the line, carrying passengers to where they wanted to go, he thought and thought about what the Really Big Surprise could be, but couldn't think of anything.

When he got to Laxey, however, he got something of a shock. Standing in the siding was a tram. A tram whom he knew, but whom he had never seen in Laxey before.

And that wasn't all. Sven looked several times to make sure he wasn't seeing things.

The tram was attached to a Horse.

While his passengers were getting off and on, Sven called across to the tram: 'Hello! Aren't you Rose? I've seen you sometimes when I've stopped at Derby Castle, haven't I?'

The little tram had been waiting rather nervously, but smiled in a friendly way. 'Yes, that's me.'

'Don't you work for the Douglas Bay Tramway?' asked Sven

Rose nodded: 'Yes, I usually take passengers along by the sea in Douglas. Today is a Day Out.'

'What are you doing here?' asked Sven.

'Practising,' said Rose shyly. 'As I'm the Bay Tramway Number 1, I've been invited to your birthday party, but I don't know your rails so I've been brought here to learn.'

'Excellent!' said Sven, 'the more trams the better. Er… but, you don't have a pole do you?' he asked, and then added hurriedly, 'I don't mean to be rude, but how will you get some of our electricity without a pole.'

Rose said cheerfully: 'you're not being rude. No, I don't have a pole. My tramway is older than yours and they hadn't really invented electricity when they built us. I don't need electricity to go along. I have Douglas.' She nodded at the horse who was placidly dozing in front of her.

'He pulls me along the seafront at Douglas, and can pull me along here too. I think the town might have been named after him.'

Sven looked impressed.

'So did Douglas pull you all the way from, er… Douglas?' asked Sven.

Rose laughed, 'No, that would be much too far.' ('*I do it three times a day*', thought Sven, and felt very important.) 'Horses are strong, but not that strong,' said Rose, 'and some of the hills would be too steep for Douglas.' ('*I don't mind the hills*', thought Sven feeling even more important.)

Rose noticed that Sven was looking a bit superior and added: 'Douglas is very good if the track gets flooded, though. He can work just as well if his feet get wet.'

Sven stopped looking superior at once. The MER trams didn't like floods *at all*. Rain was alright, but floods interfered with their electricity, and stopped them going along.

Rose smiled kindly: 'We're good at different things,' she said.

'So how did you get here?' asked Sven.

'In a big lorry,' said Rose. 'Or rather, two big lorries, one with rails on the floor for me and one with straw on the floor for Douglas. They did think about towing me behind one of you, but I haven't got the right sort of coupling (which is Tramspeak for the thing which attaches trams to trailers), so they couldn't.' Neither Rose nor Sven mentioned that going by lorry was not what Good Trams usually did. Rose was embarrassed, and Sven didn't want to be rude. Besides, this was a Special Occasion.

Then Sven suddenly realised: 'Then, YOU must be the Really Big Surprise!'

Rose frowned: 'I don't think so.'

Sven was disappointed: 'why not?'

'Well you've seen me haven't you?' said Rose. 'I can't be a Big Surprise if you've already seen me.'

Sven thought about that. Rose was right. She couldn't be the Big Surprise if everyone knew about her visit. 'Perhaps Douglas is the surprise,' he thought. Sven didn't speak Horse very well, but he had a go:

'Er… Mr Douglas?' Sven asked politely. Douglas woke up and looked round. His big brown eyes were friendly.

'Er… Mr Douglas, are you the Really Big Surprise?'

'Neigh,' said Douglas and shook his head.

'Do you know what is?'

'Neigh,' said Douglas again.

Just then the stationmaster said that Sven could carry on, so he said goodbye to Rose and Douglas and started for Ramsey with his passengers. He couldn't wait to tell the other trams.

CHAPTER 4

That night in the Derby Castle tram shed Sven told the other trams: 'I saw Rose. You know, Rose from the Douglas Bay Tramway. But she was in Laxey. She was using OUR rails!' The other trams were startled.

'She couldn't have been,' said Timothy Twenty, 'she's got no pole.'

'Oh, she had her horse with her,' explained Sven, 'he's called Douglas and she thinks the town might be named after him.' All the trams looked at each other. Then they looked at Derby. He was the Oldest Tram in the World, and was the first tram to run on their line, so he knew most about it. Eventually Ninian Nineteen asked:

'Derby, has this happened before?'

'No,' said Derby slowly. He thought a bit and then said, 'perhaps this is the Really Big Surprise.'

Sven didn't like telling Derby that he was wrong. After all, Derby was the Number 1. But Sven felt he had to:

'Rose doesn't think she's the Really Big Surprise, Mr Derby,' said Sven. 'She said she couldn't be because we all know about her now.'

'That's true,' said Joan. 'But Derby is right. We've not had horses on our line before.

'Let's hope they clean up after Douglas,' sniggered one of the trams, 'or someone might step in a Really Big Surprise.'

Derby looked disapproving, but Joan couldn't help joining in the laughter.

CHAPTER 5

As Sven was working up and down the line, he noticed something that he hadn't really thought about before. All along the line there were big poles set into the ground holding up the wire so that the trams could use it to go along. People called the wire the Overhead, but Wesley the Wire Car (Number 52) whose job it was to make sure it

worked properly, always called it the Overpole.

Some of the big poles were green, but some of them were silver. The ones in the proper Ramsey station were dark red.

Sven asked his Motorman about it: 'Why are the poles different colours? Is it something important?' Then he asked anxiously: 'Should I do something different when I go past the different colours?'

Sven's Motorman laughed: 'No, Sven, the different colours don't mean anything. The poles should really all be green – except the ones at Ramsey which were painted dark red to match the station building.'

'Then why do we have silver ones too?' asked Sven.

'Well, the poles wear out, as you know,' his Motorman replied. 'The trams go past and woggle the wire, and the poles get rained on and snowed on, and pushed about by the wind and they wear out. We don't want them to fall over, so, when the poles are too worn out to be safe, new ones are put in instead. The new poles are silver when they come from the pole factory.'

Sven thought about that and then asked: 'Why don't we paint them?'

'Oh we always mean to,' said his Motorman. 'The trouble is that there are a lot of other things which we need to do too. I mean, you wouldn't want us to be painting poles if you were ill and needed mending, would you?'

Sven agreed. He definitely wouldn't want people to be painting poles and not looking after the trams.

'And anyway,' said his Motorman, 'if there were people always painting the poles they might get in our way and we wouldn't be able to take passengers where they want to go.'

Sven looked very serious. Passengers Came First. Every good tram knew that.

Even so, Sven kept thinking about the different coloured poles. He knew that different colours weren't really important. All the trams were different colours and that didn't matter a bit. He didn't show off because he was the MER's only blue tram, for example. He smiled as he remembered how much Pam the Paddlebox wanted to be green again, but that was just Pam.

The thing to remember was that, whatever colour the trams were, they were all equally important. Well, no, Derby and Joan, the Numbers 1 and 2, were probably more important than all the others, but even so… Sven started to feel muddled.

'Perhaps they're going to paint all the poles green as the Really Big Surprise,' thought Sven. He wasn't sure though. Painting poles didn't seem quite big enough for a Really Big Surprise.

CHAPTER 6

The birthday party was getting closer and the trams still didn't know what the Really Big Surprise was.

'It's probably me,' said Van Rooj the red Post Office van, importantly, 'I always come out on special occasions.'

'Then you can't be a surprise can you?' said Pam crossly.

'Do you think I'll be allowed out too?' asked Van Goff humbly. He was the goods van, which meant that he carried parcels and luggage and bicycles. The tramway didn't need him very often, so he usually stayed in the shed. As he was dark green and almost all of the rest of the fleet wore bright colours, he was often overlooked.

'Of course you will' said Joan kindly. 'Everyone will be out for the cavalcade.'

'What's a cavalcade?' asked Twain. Some years ago Twain had been badly damaged. He was completely well now, but he didn't remember much before he had been repaired.

22

All the trams started talking at once. 'Oh it's splendid!' 'Great fun!' 'Lots of people…' 'Cameras.' 'We're all polished to look our best…'

Joan was just about to sound her whistle to shut everyone up when she caught Derby frowning at her. She smiled innocently. Sounding a whistle in the shed at night was Not Allowed, but Joan didn't always obey the rule.

'Calm down, everyone, calm down' said Derby. When the trams were quiet again, he explained: 'A cavalcade, young Twain, is a procession of trams. We go along the line together, or as near together as we can. We don't do it very often. Last time was twenty-five years ago, for our 100th birthday party, and we were all wearing different colours. Lots of people come to look at us and take photographs.'

'What, *everyone*,' said Twain, amazed. '*All* of us.' He couldn't remember seeing so many trams and trailers out together before.

'Yes,' promised Derby, 'ALL of us. At least all of us who still have wheels and can move,' he added. The trams looked sad. Most of the fleet were still around, but some had been lost in a fire in Laxey shed many years ago, and one or two hadn't been seen for ages. No-one quite knew what had happened to them. Their friends missed them.

'But,' said Twain and stopped.

'Go on,' said Joan kindly.

'But, will there be enough motormen and conductors to go around?' asked Twain. Some of the trams looked a bit worried at this. No-one wanted to miss the cavalcade but if there were not enough motormen, they might not be able to go.

'Don't worry,' said Derby. Lots of the crews who have left will come back to help out. You'll see lots of old friends.

'Perhaps that's the Really Big Surprise, then,' said Sven. But he still wasn't sure.

CHAPTER 7

At last the birthday arrived. All the trams were really excited as their motormen and conductors bathed them so that they looked their best. Lots of special things were organised, but none of them seemed to be the Really Big Surprise.

Sven saw Rose and Douglas again on his way through Laxey. She smiled at him and Sven whistled in a friendly way. He made Douglas jump.

'Sorry Mr Douglas,' he said, 'didn't you expect me to whistle?'

'Neigh,' said Douglas.

'Did you like it?' asked Sven.

'Neigh,' said Douglas again. Rose grinned at Sven and said 'perhaps that was Douglas's Really Big Surprise?' Sven knew she was pulling his wheel but didn't have time to answer.

Most of Sven's passengers got off him at Laxey and went to take photographs of the three Number 1s. Rose (with Douglas of course) was the Number 1 from the Douglas Bay Tramway. Grampian was the Number 1 from the Snaefell Mountain Railway, and the same colour as Sven. Derby was the Number 1 from the Manx Electric Railway and the Oldest Tram in the World.

The three Number 1s lined up proudly, side by side. Lots of people wanted to take photographs.

The motormen from the two electric railways, and Rose's driver, were all wearing their best uniforms. All three conductors looked very smart, and Douglas had been brushed until his coat shone.

But none of them was the Really Big Surprise.

CHAPTER 8

The birthday celebrations were going to last a week and the trams all agreed that it was a long time since they'd been so excited. They still had no idea what the Really Big Surprise was though, and none of their motormen would tell them.

On the third day of the birthday week the trams were visited by a Very Important Person. Regina the Royal Trailer said it was the King, but the trams told her that the Isle of Man didn't have a king so it couldn't be him. Sven wasn't sure what a king was, but he didn't say anything because he didn't want to look stupid.

The trams were all gathered at Derby Castle (named after the Number 1) to see the Very Important Person, and also so that the Very Important Person could see them.

As many of the trams as possible were parked on the fan (which is Tramspeak for the rails outside the shed). The rest had to stay inside the shed as there wasn't room for them all on the fan. The shed doors were left open so that they could see out.

Sven couldn't help noticing that one shed door stayed firmly closed. All the trams kept looking at it and wondering what was behind it.

The Very Important Person arrived and talked a lot. Everyone tried to be polite and listen, but it had been such an exciting day that the trams found it very hard not to doze off.

Eventually the Very Important Person stopped talking and went over to the closed shed door.

'This is a very special birthday for the Manx Electric Railway and its trams,' he said. 'We decided to do something really special to celebrate it.' He swung open the closed door and everyone peered inside.

Something whistled.
Then something moved.
Then a tram appeared.
She came slowly out into the sunshine. Her paint was gleaming, her brass was polished and her woodwork shone. She stood there proudly, beaming at them all.

They gazed back in shock.

'It's Fenella,' said Pam the Paddlebox, amazed. 'Fenella Fourteen. She arrived here at the same time as me. But… but… I haven't seen her for *ages*.'

Sven whispered something to his Motorman who nodded enthusiastically. Then Sven sounded his whistle. Joan understood straight away, and started to whistle too. Then Derby majestically joined in. One by one all the trams began to hoot, peep, toot and whistle to welcome Fenella Fourteen home. She stood there in the sunshine and beamed round at them all.

'They mended me,' Fenella said happily.

'But… where have you been?' asked Pam, bewildered.

'I've been at the back of Ramsey shed. And,' Fenella whispered, sounding scared, 'I only had wheels at One End'. All the trams gasped. They needed wheels at both ends to Go, so being Without Wheels was terrible. It meant that they couldn't Go. And, if a tram can't Go, then it isn't really a tram any more.

'But they rescued me,' said Fenella cheering up. 'They woke me up and brought me back to Derby Castle.' She looked a bit ashamed for the moment as she said in a small voice, 'I had to be brought back (sshh) by *road*.' For a moment the trams looked serious. They were always very polite to the lorries and buses which ran along the roads, but couldn't help feeling slightly superior. After all, the trams were There First. Cars of course weren't important, so were mostly ignored.

'I rode on the back of a Very Big Lorry,' said Fenella. 'I didn't feel very well *at all* – we trams carry passengers, we're not supposed to *be* passengers, and I didn't like it. I was very high up and could see our nice rails in the distance sometimes though, and that made me feel better. They brought me back to our tram shed at Derby Castle and put me at the back of the workshop.

'Then they closed the doors.'

'I was very frightened because you know what the rumours are,' said Fenella. The trams all nodded solemnly. Nobody mentioned the words Spare Parts, but they all knew stories about how bits from other trams had been taken off and reused.

'Then the Chief Engineer explained that, in honour of our 125th birthday, they were going to mend me and let me work again,' went on Fenella, 'and that's what they've been doing over the winter. And…' she beamed again, 'here I am!' All the trams whistled again and Fenella Fourteen joined in happily.

So THAT was the Really Big Surprise!